Numbers
with
Easter Eggs

1 to 25

Name:______________________

Start Date:______________________

Finish Date:______________________

Mommy & Baby Series

Book - 2

Step 1: Color the numbers.

Step 2: Color small eggs using different colors. One egg is for mommy and one is for baby.

Step 3: Color the Big Egg (inside dashed line).

Step 4: Cut it following the dashed line.

Step 5: For baby, hang or paste it in the room.

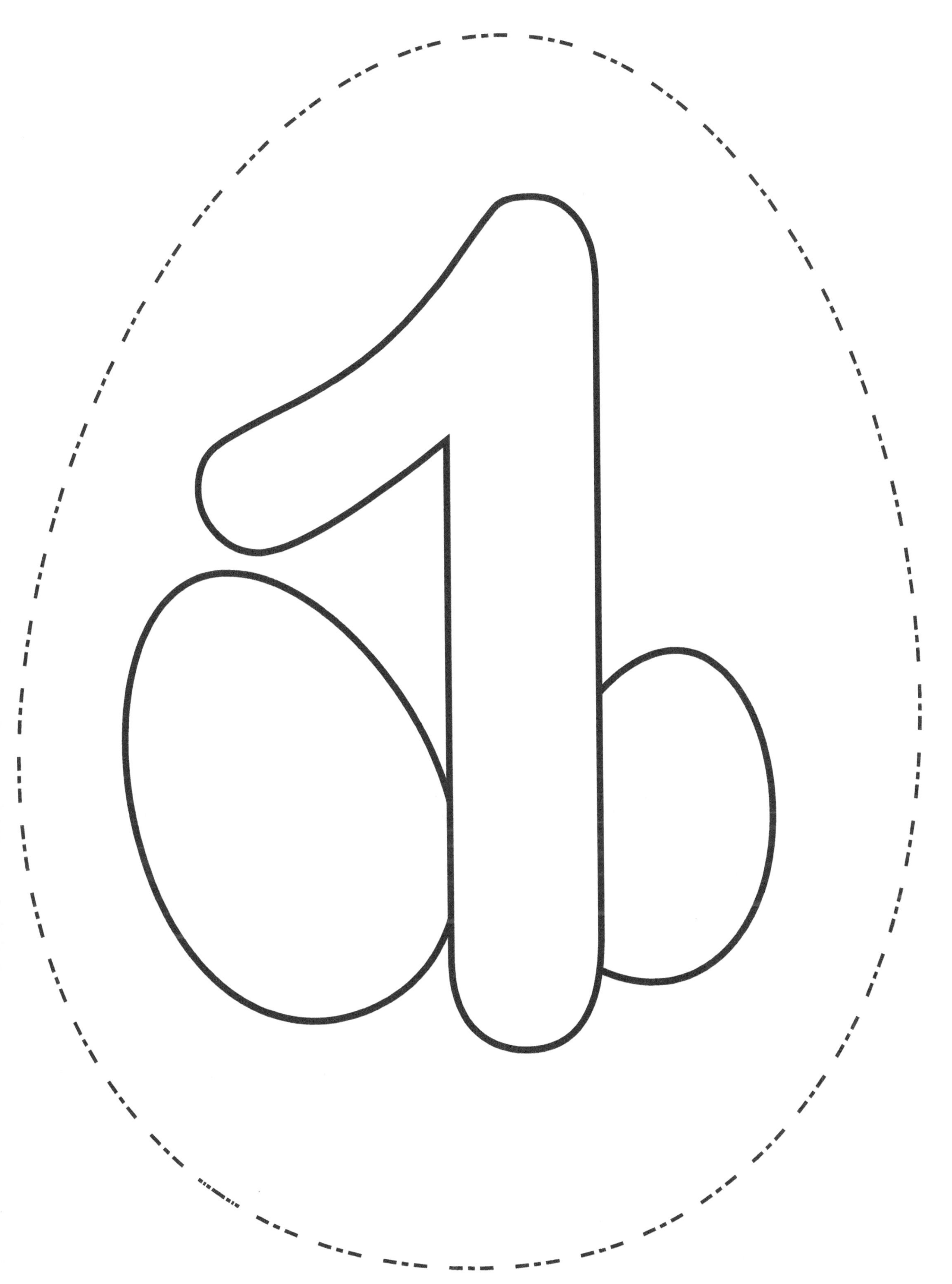

1 6 11 16 21

2 7 12 17 22

3 8 13 18 23

4 9 14 19 24

5 10 15 20 25